Be An Encourager

Diane Milnes

EnerPower Press
twww.enerpowerpress.com
(An Imprint of Energion Publications)

2011

ISBN10: 1-893729-99-0
ISBN13: 978-1-893729-99-5

Dedication

In honor of my mama,
Mary Horton,
who taught and encouraged me
and many other people at
Ancient City Baptist Church,
St. Augustine, FL.

In memory of
"Mama Gladys" Usina
who gave me alot of laughs
over the years
I took care of her.

Table of Contents

FOREWORD

The author of this work, Diane Milnes, has been personally a dear sister for nearly four years but, more importantly, has been an incredible influence to the faith of many for far longer. Diane represents multiple facets of faithfulness that are uncommon in the American *"religion"* of Christianity.

Most of us have become Christians within the American culture of "too much stuff." We attend services at churches organized under incredible prosperity with financial resources aplenty to maintain magnificent houses of "worship" with salaried staffing, fellowship rooms, gymnasiums, cafeterias, and seating. Folks can bring their praise and worship to God comfortably sheltered from the natural elements and free from the disturbances of distracting children.

In the midst of all the pomp and circumstance of religion, if one were to look closely, one might find a person or two characterized by Diane Milnes, a true believer, a worshipper, lover, and faithful individual with a history of simply trusting God in loving obedience, undaunted by the splendor of prosperity. While the organization of the church basks in the human glorification of stained glass, cushioned seating, and lofty crosses funded by faithful tithes, Diane rests with Divinely-provided contentment in a sparsely furnished, tiny trailer looking for ways to give away what remains of her little bit of post-tithe income after rent and filling her car with gas.

What characterizes Diane's love and faith? This one who has often been encouraged by Diane offers these insights into the spiritual character of Diane:

— *Humility.* Christians often debate what this quality looks like and some err in thinking too much of themselves while others err in thinking too little of themselves. Diane exemplifies Christ-like humility in that she rarely thinks *anything* of herself because she's always thinking of and praying for others.

— *Faithful.* Christians too often are praying consciously or unconsciously for the preservation of their comfort, heath, and lifestyle. Diane exemplifies Christ-likeness as she rarely seeks things from God for herself, yet her prayers never fail to remember God for His provision as she relentlessly prays for the needs of others *who already have a hundredfold more than she!*

— *Dependable.* The one writing this introduction is not found in a lot of prayer meetings; but cannot ever recall having attended a call to prayer in which Diane was not a part. Diane has long been as Henry Blackaby refers to in his study, *Experiencing God,* the "knees" of the Body of Christ, the Church.

— *Generous.* Surrounding the residence of Diane are gated resort communities housing a populous of some of the wealthiest people and families in the world. Diane will show up at a meeting with a gift designated for a local homeless shelter, a gift that to most of those seated around her would represent an amount from the dust in their pockets, but represents from Diane an amount that was meant for her own lunches for the remainder of the week.

— *Evangelical.* From her simple faith screams an incorruptible testimony that God is good always, that God's mercy and grace is wholly sufficient, and that Jesus Christ is the one and only way of salvation, deliverance, forgiveness, and reconciliation. To those looking to see Jesus Christ in action, Diane is that reflection. But, unlike most of us who like to excuse our silence with the lame words, *"my life will tell the story…",* Diane is never ashamed of the verbalized gospel message.

Diane is not eloquent or sophisticated, and she'd most likely pass through this world and its philosophies without notice or accolade. There is no doubt, however, that in God's Kingdom the name Diane Milnes is well known and applauded even daily! Diane exemplifies simple trust and faith in God and sets a high bar for those of us who call ourselves Believers.

Diane has invested her heart in this simple testimony of encouragement as she- a beggar who has found bread- hungers to see others find bread and that hope and encouragement that comes from finding the living Bread of Life.

— A "not-so-secret" Admirer

Chapter 1

Scriptures that have encouraged me

There are many words of encouragement in the Bible but I am going to share some of my favorites with you.

Barnabas was used by God in Acts 11:22-30. News had reached the church at Jerusalem that God was at work in Antioch. They sent Barnabas to Antioch to check out what was going on. When he saw what God was doing among the people of Antioch he was glad and encouraged them to follow the LORD with all their hearts. Barnabas was a good man, full of the Holy Spirit and faith. Many people were brought to the Lord through his work.

Barnabas went and found Saul in Tarsus and brought him to Antioch to minister with him for a whole year. Many people grew in the Lord through the encouragement of Barnabas and Saul. Barnabas and Saul went to the believers in Judea with an offering collected by the people of Antioch

after they heard there was going to be a
great famine.

Paul went about with his traveling com-
panions and disciples encouraging them in
the ways of the Lord. When they would be
leaving one area to go to another, Paul
would leave the people with words of encouragement. In Romans 16:1-16 Paul has
encouraging words for many men and wo-
men that were working hard in the spread
of the gospel of Christ. Verses 21-24 lists
encouraging words for the people that were
working with Paul and traveling with him.

In I Corinthians 1:4-9 Paul is encouraging the people of Corinth in their gifts
that God had given them to help them grow
in their knowledge because of the testimony about Christ being confirmed in
them. Paul encouraged them for becoming
followers of Jesus Christ.

II Corinthians 1:3-11 contains words of
encouragement. It it uplifting when we can
praise God and Jesus for having compassion on us and that He gives us comfort no
matter what we are going through. God
cares for us so that we can care for others
in the same way. We are encouraged to pray
for people in their times of need. We are

comforted when we see these needs met.

Paul encouraged the Corinthians to get their promised offering gathered ahead of his arrival. These verses have raised me up many times.

II Corinthians 9:6 reminds us that if we sow sparingly we will also reap sparingly, and whoever sows generously will also reap generously.God loves a cheerful giver as we are told in verse seven. Your generous offerings will bring thanksgiving to God. People will pray for you because of how God has blessed you.

Ephesians 5:19-21 is another favorite passage of mine.

> *Speak to one another with psalms, hymns, and spiritual songs. Sing and make music in your heart to the Lord, always giving thanks to God the Father for everything, in the name of our Lord Jesus Christ. Submit to one another out of reverence for Christ.*

I know what joy and peace I feel in my life from hearing or singing praise to God in my patient's room, in my home, in my car and at church services. When I am having a bad day, I turn to God in praise and music and my outlook on the day will totally change.

In Philippians 2:1-11 we find many words of encouragement. We are encouraged to be in unity in Christ Jesus. We are called to be an imitator of Christ; following His example. We are to share God's love, being one in spirit and purpose. We find comfort in God's love, and fellowship with the Spirit, tenderness and compassion. Follow Jesus Christ's examples. Jesus was a humble man while on earth even though he came down from his throne in heaven. God exalted him and raised him up. To God be the glory for great things he has done.

In Paul's words in I Thessalonians 1, we are encouraged to lift each other up in prayer. Sometimes God will bring people to your mind that are not initially in your thoughts. Maybe they are in need at that very moment. I was sitting in a different place in my home today and I saw a picture of a person I had not thought of for a while. Therefore, I lifted that person up in prayer.

In I Thessalonians 2-3, we are told to be encouragers, comforters, and diligent servants of God who calls us into his kingdom and glory. Since Paul and his fellowmen in the gospel could not get back to minister to the Thessalonians, they just sent Timothy. He went back to strengthen and encourage the people in their faith. Timothy was able to bring back words of encouragement to Paul and the others that the people were still walking in faith.

In Titus chapter 2, I feel we are encouraged to help those who are younger than we are. We need to be a good example of how to live and minister. There were people in my life as a child that I looked up to for guidance and encouragement in the ways of God. I try to be an encourager to younger adults as well as children I meet and minister to.

As Paul encouraged Philemon to be active in sharing his faith so that others can come to know the way to Christ, also we are encouraged to share our faith to lead others to a saving knowledge of Jesus Christ.

Hebrews 10:23-25 —

Let us hold unswervingly to the hope we profess, for he who promised is faithful. And let us consider how we may spur one another on toward love and good deeds. Let us not give up meeting together, as

some are in the habit of doing, but let us
encourage one another - and all the more
as you see the Day approaching.

We are called by God in these words of scripture to help each other minister and increase our faith. Spur others on toward love and good deeds.

I encourage people to continue to be faithful in church and ministry. I know I feel closer to God when I am in fellowship and ministry in church and with fellow Christian friends. Those times are a vital part of my week.

In I John 4:7-21 we are encouraged to love one another, for love comes from God. If we are born of God, we love and know God. If we do not love, we do not know love because God is love. God loved us so much that He sent his Son to die for us for our sins. That is great love! Because God loved us this much we ought to love others also.

Chapter 2

Encouragers in my life as a child

I am so grateful to God for people that encouraged me when I was a child. Some of these people I kept in touch with as an adult to let them know how they influenced my life in Christ.

Two of these people that are in my mind most often when I think about my childhood are Mr. and Mrs. Al Hess. They were my first Sunday School teachers that I can remember having at Ancient City Baptist Church. I credit them with being the first people to encourage me and others in our class to be supporters of missionaries and also to *be* missionaries. We had a missionary to Mexico come speak at our church. Mr. and Mrs. Hess started a missionary support box. The box sat on the piano in our Sunday School department. We would talk about missions a lot and put our small change in the box. Every so often, they would let us know how much was in the box and that we would send our missionary her support. I know adults had to be putting dollars into the box because there would be more than our change could have added up to.

Even after I was no longer in the same Sunday School class I would still go talk to Mr. and Mrs. Hess. Sometimes I was allowed to sit with them during church. When I was an adult and had moved away, I would still go visit Mr. Hess or call him on the phone when I was in town. I talked to him about how he and his wife had encouraged me to be a missionary or a supporter of other missionaries when I could not go on missionary journeys.

I remember also Mrs. Hollingsworth who taught our Sunday School class *"Jesus Loves Me"*, *"Jesus Loves The Little Children"*, and other children's songs. I have been singing these songs all my life in times of needing ministry from God and many times of teaching and ministering to other people. I talked to Mrs. Hollingsworth at the funeral of Mama Gladys (a patient that I cared for) a few weeks ago. I thanked her for teaching me those simple children's songs so many years ago. I also shared with her that I sang these songs to Mama Gladys many times over the seven years that I cared for her. Sometimes she would sing the songs with me. I shared with her how the words of *"Jesus Loves Me"* would bring peace to Mama Gladys when she would be in pain between doses of morphine. I would be amazed at how God was working in her life as she waited for God to take her home. Some of the family members got to witness the peace that this song would bring to her. I hope and pray that these songs will continue to bring encouragement and peace to this family and many others also.

My fourth and fifth grade teacher at Evelyn Hamblem Elementary School encouraged me all my life. I went to visit my former teacher today. At age 97, she could not remember a lot but I told her how she encouraged me starting with being my teacher in fourth and fifth grade. She said she was so blessed to know that because of her I continued in school. She did not remember, but I used to go visit her at her house when I needed encouragement as a teenager. She lived a couple houses down from Ancient City Baptist Church. After I moved from St. Augustine, I kept in touch with her through my sister, Doris. They went to the same church. When I was a missionary with Teen Missions International, I would send her my newsletters. After I moved back to St. Augustine I went to see her and shared my mission pictures from Hungary/Ukraine. Today I had grandchildren pictures to share with her. She said to hurry up and write my book and get it published so she can read it before she dies.

Miss Alden was my favorite teacher in my senior year at St. Augustine High School. I would go to her class after school a lot of the days. She would help me not only with English but also with my other classes I needed help with. My grades improved a lot that year. I also used to bring her roses from my rose bush. I think my roses bloomed better that school year than any other time. I am glad I got to know Miss Alden that year. She retired at our graduation and died a few weeks later.

Mr. Richard Bassett was my history teacher in twelfth grade. He encouraged me a lot by helping me with all my home work if Miss Alden was not available. I also got encouragement from him because I needed to make a certain grade on my final exam to bring my grade up to a "C" so that I could graduate. Mr. Bassett let me take the exam over twice in one day. I finally passed high enough to graduate the morning of graduation. I was so grateful for him doing that. Without that help I would have needed to finish at adult education. I probably would have been too discouraged to go on.

Reverend Carson Brittain meant a lot in my life. Reverend Brittain was my last pastor at Ancient City Baptist Church before I moved from St. Augustine in 1973. I used to call him Rev. C.B. I stayed in contact with him for nearly thirty five years. I shared mission pictures with him many times over the years. I remember I stopped at his house in Lake City, Florida before I left for a Ukraine/Hungary mission trip. He had just gotten out of the hospital. He said it was the first time to come out of his bedroom in pajamas to receive a visitor. I told him it was all right. When I got back from my mission trip he and his wife, Tiny, had moved to a nursing home. I never saw them again. I am so glad that I stopped to see them before my mission trip. I am also very glad that he and Tiny were a part of my life.

My mama, Mary Horton, was not only an encourager to our family, she was obed-

ient to God in seeing that people had rides
to church and Sunday School, choir, train-
ing union, and sword drill team. She taught
many years of Sunday School and Girls
Auxiliary (G.A.'s) at Ancient City Baptist
Church. She also encouraged my sisters and
me to learn and excel in the things that were
required for advancing in G.A.'s. We stud-
ied a lot about missions and missionaries in
our classes. When we were adults going on
mission trips, she helped us financially and
prayerfully. She even helped with Elizabeth,
my daughter, going on missions. She took
care of grandchildren and a great-grandson,
making sure they got to church when they
were under her care. She has been in a rest
home with Alzheimer's disease for many
years. I really miss the Mama that was able
to minister to all of us. I know that God is
taking care of her spirit. I am thankful to
God for that.

Here is what Mama wrote in the 100
year anniversary book from Ancient City
Baptist Church:

> I thought of writing about my fa-
> vorite pastor, but couldn't decide
> who was my favorite; each was a

unique personality with different talents.

God in His great wisdom knew what we needed each time and sent the right person for that time. Each has a special place in my heart. Thank you T.J. Powers, Paul Carmichael, Carson Brittain, and Bobby Musselwhite.

Then, I thought of the spooky Halloween parties we used to have in the dark, damp upstairs of the old Barcelona Hotel, and the beautiful Christmas parties we had in the elegant but rundown ballroom. This was a very happy time in my life as I made friendships that will last a lifetime.

Happiness and contentment would not be complete without service, so I remember my wonderful years as a leader in Sunbeams, G.A's, and Y.W.A's. I feel great pride as I see the still growing, productive Christian lives of so many of my girls.

Of course, my favorite memories would have to include Sunday

School whether as a class member
or a teacher. I'm looking forward to
many more years of planting, water-
ing, and reaping for God's Kingdom and Ancient City Baptist
Church.[1]

Mama's verse: Psalm 50:10 says, *"For every
beast of the forest is Mine, and the cattle on a thou-
sand hills."* So many times Mama said that
verse when we would see all the cows in the
fields near Dowling Park, Florida. I used
this verse concerning a financial need from
time to time because I could rely on God
to supply my needs. God could sell a cow
if needed.

---

1   *The Long Road With God: A Living History of Ancient
City Baptist Church 1887-1987.* E.O. Painter Printing
Company. DeLeon Springs, FL. 1987.

Chapter 3

Encouragement from the Psalms

Psalms has a lot of words to encourage us. I find great joy in singing praises to God. Some of these words come directly from the book of Psalms. See Psalm 8:1. *"O LORD, our Lord, how majestic is Your name in all the earth, You have set Your glory above the heavens."* This is one of the psalms I sing. Psalms 42:1-2 *"As the deer pants for streams of water, so my soul pants for you, O God."* When I sing these verses I feel encouraged to be closer to God through Bible study. When we get our spiritual sponge refilled with God then we can go and encourage others with God's word and time of ministry. After our spiritual sponge gets squeezed out we can go back to God for another fill up. [This sponge illustration I use from a sermon some years ago but I think it is an encouragement to me and others.]

I have cried a lot recently about the long hours I have spent caring for my patient as she was coming to the end of her life. I am encouraged as I know that God is with us. I have thought about the words of Psalms 56:8-9. I just read them this morning. *"Record my lament; list my tears on Your scroll— are they not in Your record? Then my enemies will turn back when I call for help."* By this I will know that God is for me. I know that God is with us even in this sad and tiring time the enemy is at work. God will see us through.

November 6 at 4:00 a.m. Mama Gladys entered her Heavenly rest. Praise God! I was reading Psalms the last 45 minutes of her life. I closed my Bible at the exact minute she died. I closed with Psalms 89:52 which says: *"Praise be to the LORD forever! Amen and Amen."*

The next day when I was reading in Psalms 92 I received encouraging words from verse 4. *"For you make me glad by your deeds, O Lord; I sing for joy at the works of your hands."* Verses like that remind me of Mama Gladys, Joy (her daughter, and I being together. Joy had given me a statue of Joseph, Mary and the baby Jesus. It had Luke 1:14 on it. *"And they shalt have joy and gladness, and many shall rejoice at his name."* That verse reminds me of Joy, Gladys, grandson Luke, and me rejoicing in God together.

Psalms 100:2 tells us to *"Worship the LORD with gladness; come before him with joyful songs."* At church yesterday I was worshiping in song pretty easily until we started singing a song that Mama Gladys and I listened to and that I sang for her. I cried a lot during that song. Friends nearby hugged me and cried with me. I know God will see all of us through times of many tears for the family that is left behind. We can rejoice with God for family that is in Heaven where there are no more tears, suffering or pain. Praise God!

Psalms 134 is encouraging to me as it leads me to praise the LORD. Verse 2 says we are to *"Lift up your hands in the sanctuary and praise the LORD."* God inhabits the praises of His people.

Chapter 4

Encouraging Testimonies

This chapter contains testimonies from people who have been encouraged by someone or that God has used to be an encourager.

Here is a testimony I got from Bruce Curtis, a man in my life group at Anastasia Baptist Church.

AN OASIS IN THE DESERT

BY BRUCE CURTIS

When I think of an oasis, I think of palm-tree shaded, crystal-clear pool of fresh water in the middle of a hostile, desolate, and unfriendly desert, like a tiny piece of heaven in the middle of hell. I see an oasis as an unbelievably awesome place of rest along the path of an arduous journey and as a place where cleansing and refreshing is found by dusty and thirsty travelers. An oasis is a place where one will be tempted to stay, but knows he must move on.

When we're lost and about to give up, when we think we've reached the absolute end of our endurance, just when we've concluded there is no hope, no way out, the Lord provides an oasis. I'll remember always one such oasis on my journey. It was in the home of the Cutler family.

We'd made a major life decision. Sell the house in New York abandoning snow blowers, parkas and mittens, and move to St. Augustine, Florida. We began the slow process in June of some painting, wallpapering, and general fix-up stuff. Yvette began packing non- essentials. Unexpectedly in mid-August a neighbor made an offer to purchase our house. We were unprepared, surprised and pleased. Yvette made a trip to Florida, found a house and I flew down to sign purchase contracts. I would transfer with my company and

Yvette would have no difficulty finding a job in medical billing. This was going to be a slam-dunk. Or, so we thought..............

There was one onslaught after another. The time table and schedule of events we'd worked out was obliterated to the point where there was but one decision that would mean certainty- that was to pull the plug on the whole plan to move. Any decision other than to pull the plug left us without knowing if we could buy a home in Florida, find a job in Florida, have a place to take a truckload of household stuff. We chose not to pull the plug but, instead, to pray, trust God for the outcome, and "pull the trigger".

I'd always thought that once a decision was made to trust God that one is immediately overwhelmed with a euphoric sense of peace about everything and one's mind was empty of even one single concern. Well, maybe that is so for some folks. It was not that way for me. I was assaulted by anguish, fear, worry, and distress as one crisis followed another. At the end of a very long Saturday, after the hard-working friends from church had helped load the moving truck, I accepted the offer of some old friends in Lake George to spend Saturday night at their home. Sunday I returned to begin the final cleaning in anticipation of closing and heading for Florida Tuesday afternoon. I found myself wondering around a cold, empty house- alone because Yvette (my wife) was already in Florida job hunting. I'd reached the end of my endurance. One "what if" situation after another dominated my thoughts and my insides churned with worry and anxiety.

The ringing phone echoed in the empty house. Connie and Jack Cutler invited me to come for dinner with their family and spend the night. She had some insight into the difficulties that we'd experienced along the way and she, Jack and the kids had been praying for us.

I spent Sunday and Monday night and part of Tuesday with the Cutler family and there I encounter Jesus. It was without question my desperately needed oasis. I rested. I drank from God-inspired encouragement. I was rejuvenated, filled with faith and edified. I was cleansed of worry and torment. I was freed from the burden of "what ifs". I was refocused and reminded of the fact that in all that had transpired, God had known all along would happen. We'd planned as best as we could on a limited knowledge we had. We couldn't have predicted the September 11th attack that would rob us of our savings; we couldn't have foreseen the engineers report that severely diminished the value of our home sale; nor could we have known beforehand of the countless delays and awkward lack of communication concerning the process of sale. And the trial didn't end with the closing on the house. Obstacles, challenges and delays continued even after we drove to Florida.

My "oasis experience" with the Cutler family was arranged by the Lord. He knew how weary I'd become and knew the difficult struggle yet ahead. Through the ministry of the Cutler family the Lord took away the burdensome load of worry and stress that I was carrying and gave me the strength to endure what would come.

"Praise", I think, is the heart-felt expression of our awe and gratitude for the fact that One so lofty and mighty as He cares for one so lowly and helpless as we. I praise you, Father.

– Bruce Curtis 2001

As one is encouraged, then one becomes an encourager. I praise God for Bruce talking to me after "Experiencing God" class one night. I had mentioned several weeks in a row that I felt God wanted me to find a place of my own for rest on the weekends when I was not working. I told classmates that I felt fear that things would not work out right with the extra expenses of rent and a place to stay. After Bruce prayed with me and told me to get going on what I felt God was leading me I felt more peace. I went out riding around and found this nice little trailer park. I came in to talk to the landlady who said there were no vacancies. By the time I got home she called and said someone came to say they were moving. The next weekend I came to look at the mobile home that would become my home. I kept saying "WOW." Everything was so neat. The next weekend friends from church had gathered unused items and helped me move in that first day. I was so excited to see how God had everything under control.

My sister, Doris, always inspired me to publish the tracts that I wrote. I am so glad she did. She was really excited for me when I told her God wanted me to write this book. I was encouraged by her as she went ahead with the plans to do a Spanish vacation Bible school. Before it started she found out she needed heart surgery and that she had breast cancer as well as other medical problems. Now I am going to share with you what she wrote for my book. She is still encouraging and inspiring people.

I believe God has gifted me in exhortation or with encouraging others. The opportunities that God has put before me have been the young and the aging. I recently organized and participated in a youth mission trip where the group led a Vacation Bible School for a Hispanic church. Each morning the youth and the leaders were required to spend 20-30 minutes in quietness with God and His Word. One group of high school youth kept turning on the radio during their designated quiet time. Each day, I would tell them to turn off the "noise" so they could listen to God. The conversation would end with "I can listen better with the music on." It wasn't until the end of the summer that one of the youth in "that group" came to me and told me that she now understood why she was to turn off the noise. She had discovered that she had to "be fully still and quiet to listen to God." She shared that

God was calling her in to the ministry [16 years old]. She recently
preached in our church. My soul
was "still" as I listened to her sermon.

Psalm 46:10a *(KJV) Be still, and
know that I am God.*

Exodus 14:13 *(KJV) And Moses
said unto the people, fear ye not, stand
still, and see the salvation of the LORD,
which he will shew to you today: for the
Egyptians whom ye have seen today, ye
shall see them again no more forever.*

Numbers 9:8 (KJV) *And Moses
said unto them, stand still, and I will
hear what the LORD will command concerning you.*

1 Samuel 9:27 (KJV) *And as they
were going down to the end of the city,
Samuel said to Saul, Bid the servant pass
on before us, [and he passed on], but
stand thou still a while, that I may shew
thee the word of God.*

Psalm 4:4 (KJV) *Stand in awe, and
sin not: commune with your heart upon
your bed, and be still.*

— Doris Murdoch

When I was reading the book of Ruth recently I felt my daughter, Elizabeth, is like Ruth to me. Even though Ruth had lost her husband and chose to leave her family to be with Naomi, God used her obedience to bless Ruth and Naomi. Elizabeth has not lost her husband, but I think of her as my "Ruth" because she has remained strong through her many trials with surgeries and chemo for her cancer and with Eliza being sick. She is also busy being an elementary school teacher and pastor's wife, and mother of two small children. I believe God has blessed her to be able to carry on and still care about her mother's pain and sorrow that is not as bad as what she has gone through. She gives me strength and joy to carry on.

I thank God for both my children and my grandchildren. I am also encouraged to read the words of 3 John 1:2 which says, *"Dear friends, I pray that you may enjoy good health and that all may go well with you, even as your soul is getting along well."* Thank you, God, that I was able to encourage Elizabeth when she was sick. We are good encouragers for each other. I think God will continue to use

Elizabeth as an encourager for people who are going through hard times.

Pastor Dan just got back from Chad, Africa, where he went to help his brother and sister-in-law do some repairs and updates on the house and medical clinic they run. He spoke about his trip at church yesterday and I was reminded anew of our call to encourage the workers that the harvest fields of souls for Jesus are ripe. We need to sow and reap the harvest now. Also I had just felt called to go back to volunteer at Teen Missions International in Merritt Island, Florida this summer so I called and asked for the paperwork to fill out. At Teen Missions this summer children, teens and adult leaders will meet together and train for going all over the world to preach the gospel and win souls for Jesus. We will have opportunities to counsel with the people who come forward for ministry time in the nightly rallies where missionaries share their experiences and have an invitation. Some of the people will come to receive Jesus as Lord. Others will come to share troubles they may have had at home or with fellow leaders and teammates. It is great to minister to these people. Boot Camp is a very hard experience to go through but it is all worth it when you see all the people as they load the buses to go all over the world to do their mission projects that have been set up. They have building projects, medical and evangelism projects.

Even if I never get to other parts of the world, I feel I have children all over the world that got to hear the gospel and accept Jesus as Lord because I got to encourage other missionaries to go and reap a harvest.

More inspirational reading from Energion Publications

What is God calling you to do?

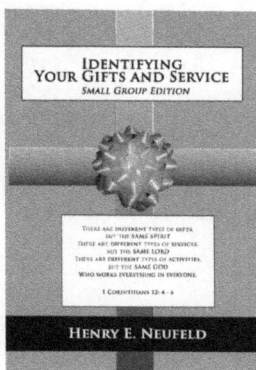

Are you looking for the place where God wants you to serve in the body of Christ? Author Henry Neufeld believes that the Holy Spirit is the best guide to finding the gifts God has given you and putting them to use in service. This study is designed for church groups who want to help one another hear from the Holy Spirt and find the best place to serve. It can also be used by individuals in cooperation with their community.

For Christians who grieve

Teacher, writer, and retired Hospice nurse Jody Neufeld combines her skills with social worker Janet Wilkie to invite Christians to acknowledge their grief and work through to find the candle of light. This book never tries to minimize the pain of loss but always points toward new hope. If you ever encounter anyone who is dealing with grief, this book is a must read!

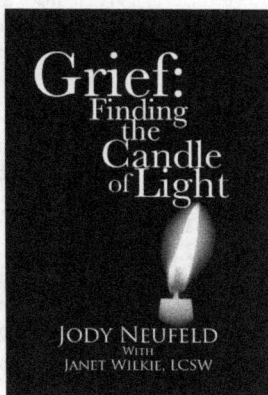

More from Energion Publications

Personal Study

Christian Archy	$9.99
Christianity and Secularism	$16.99
Evidence for the Bible	$16.99
Holy Smoke, Unholy Fire	$14.99
Not Ashamed of the Gospel	$12.99
The Jesus Paradigm	$17.99
The Messiah and His Kingdom to Come (B&W)	$19.99
The Politics of Witness	$9.99
Ultimate Allegiance	$9.99
What's In A Version?	$12.99
When People Speak for God	$17.99

Christian Living

Daily Devotions of Ordinary People–Extraordinary God	$19.99
Directed Paths	$7.99
Grief: Finding the Candle of Light	$8.99
I Want to Pray	$7.99
Soup Kitchen for the Soul	$12.99
Victim No More	$12.99
Words of Life, Light, and Love	$7.99

Bible Study

Ephesians: A Participatory Study Guide	$9.99
Identifying Your Gifts and Service: Small Group	$12.99
Learning and Living Scripture	$12.99
Revelation: A Participatory Study Guide	$9.99
St. Luke: A Participatory Study Guide	$8.99
To the Hebrews: A Participatory Study Guide	$9.99
Why Four Gospels?	$11.99

Theology

Finding My Way in Christianity	$16.99
God's Desire for the Nations	$18.99
Operation Olive Branch	$16.99
Out of This World	$24.99

Generous Quantity Discounts Available
P.O. Box 841
Gonzalez, FL 32560
Website: http://energionpubs.com
Phone: (850) 525-3916